Look Inside a
Tree

Richard Spilsbury

Raintree is an imprint of Capstone Global Library Limited, a company incorporated in England and Wales having its registered office at 7 Pilgrim Street, London, EC4V 6LB – Registered company number: 6695582

To contact Raintree please phone 0845 6044371, fax + 44 (0) 1865 312263, or email myorders@raintreepublishers.co.uk. Customers from outside the UK please telephone +44 1865 312262.

Text © Capstone Global Library Limited 2013
First published in hardback in 2013
The moral rights of the proprietor have been asserted.

Edited by Rebecca Rissman, Dan Nunn, and John-Paul Wilkins
Designed by Steve Mead
Original illustrations © Capstone Global Library Ltd 2013
Illustrations by Gary Hanna
Picture research by Ruth Blair
Production by Alison Parsons
Originated by Capstone Global Library Ltd
Printed in China

ISBN 978 1 406 25130 2 (hardback)
16 15 14 13 12
10 9 8 7 6 5 4 3 2 1

British Library Cataloguing in Publication Data
Spilsbury, Richard.
Look inside a tree.
577.3-dc23
A full catalogue record for this book is available from the British Library.

Acknowledgements
We would like to thank the following for permission to reproduce photographs: iStockphoto pp. 24 (© Martin Pot), 25 (© Michael Pettigrew), 27 (© DAMIAN KUZDAK); Naturepl pp. 9 (© Andrew Cooper), 19 (© Ingo Arndt), 26 right (© Andy Rouse); Shutterstock pp. 5 left (© Bruce MacQueen), 5 right (© Marek CECH), 6 (© Gorilla), 7 (© lafoto), 8 (© Virunja), 11 (© D. Kucharski & K. Kucharska), 12 (© jack53), 13 (© mlorenz), 14 (© FloridaStock), 15 (© Erik Mandre), 17 (© alslutsky), 18 (© Sergey Toronto), 20 (© Mark Bridger), 21 (© peresanz), 23 (© fotosav), 26 left (© visceralimage), 28, 29 (© Smit).

Cover photograph of a may-bug grub (*Melolontha vulgaris*) reproduced with permission of Shutterstock (© fotosav).

We would like to thank Michael Bright and Diana Bentley for their invaluable help in the preparation of this book.

Every effort has been made to contact copyright holders of any material reproduced in this book. Any omissions will be rectified in subsequent printings if notice is given to the publisher.

Disclaimer
All the internet addresses (URLs) given in this book were valid at the time of going to press. However, due to the dynamic nature of the internet, some addresses may have changed, or sites may have changed or ceased to exist since publication. While the author and publisher regret any inconvenience this may cause readers, no responsibility for any such changes can be accepted by either the author or the publisher.

Contents

Some words are shown in bold, **like this**. You can find out what they mean by looking in the glossary.

Amongst the branches

A tree is a **habitat**. It provides different animals with food and **shelter**. Some animals live and feed mostly amongst the branches of a tree.

Tits are small, busy birds that hop along branches looking for food. Tits eat **insects**, **caterpillars**, spiders, and berries. They make **nests** and lay eggs in holes in trees.

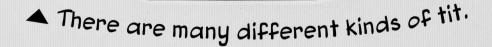

▲ There are many different kinds of tit.

A honeybee flies to a tree and walks along the branches. It sucks up sweet **nectar** from flowers. Its long tongue is hollow and works like a drinking straw!

▼ This honeybee is feeding on a tree flower.

▲ Honeybee swarms contain thousands of bees.

Swarms of honeybees sometimes make **nests** on tree branches. They use nectar to make honey in the nest. They store the honey to eat in winter when there are not many flowers about.

The grey squirrel is a **mammal** that spends most of its life up trees. It uses its strong teeth to feed on nuts and seeds. The squirrel's long, bushy tail helps it to balance as it leaps from branch to branch.

Squirrels collect food from the branches. ▶

▲ Baby squirrels huddle together to stay warm.

Female squirrels make **nests** amongst the branches. Baby squirrels are safe and warm in a nest. They only come out to eat nuts once their teeth have grown.

In the trunk

Some animals live for part of the time inside a tree **trunk**. Others search for animals to eat under the **bark** of trees.

Bark beetles bite through tree bark to eat the soft wood underneath. They also lay eggs under bark. **Larvae** that **hatch** out of the eggs eat the wood, too.

▲ Bark beetles eat wood from tree trunks.

Barn owls make **nests** in holes in tree **trunks**. The **female** owl sits on the eggs to keep them warm until the babies **hatch** out. The **male** owl catches and brings her food.

▼ This barn owl is peering out from its nest.

▲ Barn owls fly silently.

Barn owls eat mice, frogs, and other small animals. They sit and listen for **prey** scurrying on the ground. Then they swoop down to catch it.

Woodpeckers ▶
have heavy,
pointed beaks.

Woodpeckers
peck fast to make
holes in tree **trunks**.
Then they make their
nests inside. Adult birds
will attack owls and other
birds that try to eat eggs
or chicks from their nest.

Woodpeckers grip tree trunks using their strong **talons**. They poke their sharp beaks under the **bark** to feel for **insects** to eat. Their long, sticky tongues pick up the insects they find.

This **woodpecker** is ▶ feeling for insects with its tongue.

Around the base

Some smaller animals crawl up on to trees around the base. Other larger animals stand by trees and nibble at parts of the **trunk** they can reach.

Holly blue butterflies fly around trees. **Females** lay eggs on ivy that grows up tree trunks. Green **caterpillars** then **hatch** out of the eggs and eat ivy buds, berries, and leaves.

▲ Holly blue butterflies have stripy **antennae**.

A ladybird is a kind of beetle. Birds eat a lot of beetles, but they usually leave ladybirds alone. The ladybird's bright colours warn birds that they taste nasty!

▼ Red and black colours are a warning signal.

Some ladybirds ▶
huddle together
in cracks in tree
trunks when it
gets cold.

Ladybirds crawl along
tree **trunks** looking
for small **insects** to eat.
Many ladybirds sleep
in gaps under the **bark**
during winter when it is too
cold to find much food.

Some deer live in woodlands. They feed on buds, leaves, nuts, and berries. In winter, deer sometimes eat the **bark** off trees when other food is hard to find.

▼ Fallow deer are always alert to danger.

The antlers ▶
of male
deer can
grow very
large.

antlers

Young **males**
scratch their new
antlers against tree
trunks. This rubs off
the skin that protects
the antlers while
they grow. But it can
damage some trees.

Amongst the roots

Many animals find **shelter** and food in the ground beneath a tree. They live in the soil and dead leaves among the **roots**.

Some beetles lay their eggs in the soil amongst tree roots. Curled, white **larvae hatch** out of the eggs and eat the roots. They grow and change into beetles.

▲ Beetle larvae eat and eat so they can grow.

Many millipedes live amongst tree **roots**. They mostly come out at night to chomp dead leaves. Millipedes don't see well so they feel their way along using their **antennae**.

▼ A millipede on the move!

antenna

▲ Millipedes come in many different colours.

Millipedes are long, thin animals with many legs. All of their little legs move quickly to help them crawl through soil. When scared, millipedes curl up tight.

Badgers often dig large holes to live in beneath tree **roots**. The roots hold up the roofs of their **dens**. They stay in the dens in the day and come out at dusk to feed and play.

▼ The American badger (left) and European badger (right) are slightly different colours.

▲ Badgers are shy, and try to avoid humans.

Badgers use their tough claws to dig out dens and food from the soil. They have wide, flat teeth to chew worms and **larvae**. They also eat frogs, slugs, and other small animals.

Tree habitats

Spring and summer are the seasons when many trees have leaves and flowers. Many animals visit trees because there is lots of food to eat. Most baby animals are born at this time, too.

▼ A tree in summer.

▲ A tree in winter.

In winter, many trees lose their leaves. The branches are bare and the ground is cold. Fewer animals visit trees and some sleep under ground in **nests** and **dens** waiting for spring to come.

Glossary

antennae (singular: antenna) thin parts on the heads of some animals, including beetles and lobsters, that are used to feel and touch

antler bony body part that grows on a male deer's head

bark tough outer covering of a tree trunk and branches

caterpillar young stage in the life cycle of a butterfly or moth

den hidden home or resting place of some animals, such as badgers or bears

dusk time of day just before night

female sex of an animal or plant that is able to produce eggs or seeds. Females are the opposite sex to males.

habitat place where particular types of living things are likely to live. For example, polar bears live in snowy habitats and camels live in desert habitats.

hatch come out of an egg

insect type of small animal that has three body parts, six legs, and usually wings. Ants and dragonflies are types of insect.

larvae young of some animals, such as insects

male sex of an animal or plant that is unable to produce eggs or seeds. Males are the opposite sex to females.

mammal animal that has hair and feeds its babies with milk from the mother. Humans and squirrels are types of mammal.

nectar sweet liquid made by flowers to attract insects and other animals

nest place where a bird or other animal lays eggs or cares for its young. Nests are often made from twigs or grass.

prey animal that is caught and eaten by another animal

root underground part of a plant that takes in water and useful substances from the soil

shelter place that provides protection from danger or bad weather

swarm large group of flying insects

talon claw of a bird

trunk part of a tree above the ground, that supports its branches

Find out more

Books

Baby Animals in Forest Habitats (Habitats of Baby Animals), Bobbie Kalman (Crabtree Publishing, 2011)

Forests (Habitat Survival), Claire Llewellyn (Raintree, 2012)

Rotten Logs and Forest Floors (Horrible Habitats), Sharon Katz Cooper (Raintree, 2010)

Websites

Click on the spider and become a woodland explorer at:
http://www.naturegrid.org.uk/woodland/ woodexplore.html

Find out about 10 unusual animals that live in trees at:
http://animal.discovery.com/tv/a-list/creature- countdowns/treehuggers/treehuggers.html

Watch a video clip of a British woodland at:
http://www.bbc.co.uk/learningzone/clips/ a-british-woodland-habitat/8966.html

Index